MW00528696

HOW BIBLE
LEAD ME TO
ISLAM

First published in Malaysia by
Tertib Publishing
23-2 Jalan PJS 5/30
Petaling Jaya Commercial City (PJCC)
46150 Petaling Jaya, Selangor
Malaysia

Tel: +603 7772 3156

First Edition: February 2020

© Yusha Evans 2020
All Rights Reserved.

ISBN: 978-967-2420-05-7

Cover design: Ahmad Zahin Zulkipli
Transcription: Hanis Hanani Mohammad Tahir
Typesetting & Layout: Ainul Syuhada
Printed by: Firdaus Press Sdn. Bhd.

Contents

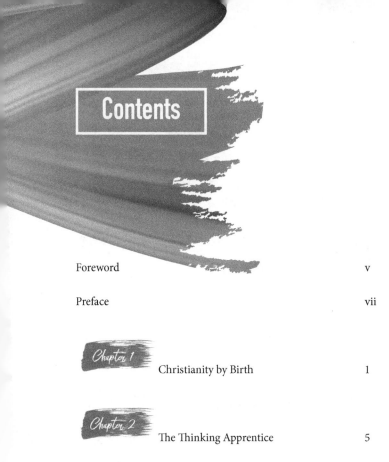

Foreword

Ever thought of being born and raised in a certain religion to be a coincident? For some, religion was determined since they were in their mother's womb while some are saved by the grace of God. The idea of being born with the religion or beliefs of the family becomes a norm; constantly being passed down as if it is inherited. However, the individual may have not decided to practice the faith for themselves. This is where *hidayah* – guidance comes in. Allah created each human being with the capability of thinking and analysing to be used for decision making; especially to decide on one's faith.

Yusha Evans is a South Carolinian, born and raised in a conservative Christian home. He shared his journey of discovering and questioning the messages from various religion which reverted him to Islam. With years of studying various religion, psychology major, master's degree in the field of Islamic sciences and worldwide qualifications, his intention is to share the message of Islam to those who are in search of the truth. He is a living example of faith is not inheritable. Therefore ask ourselves, is the way we are practicing faith merely handed down or is it out of rightful reasoning?

"And of His signs is [that] He shows you the lightening [causing] fear and aspiration, and He sends down rain from the sky by which He brings to life the earth after its lifelessness. Indeed in that are signs for a people who use reason." (Surah Ar-Rum: Verse 24)

Tertib Publishing | tertib.press

Preface

I greet my brothers and sisters with the greeting of peace, *assalamualaikum warahmatullahi wabarakatuh*. My name is Yusha Evans. I came to Islam in 1998 and I did not change my name. Yusha is just the Arabic form of Joshua, which is my birth name. I did not change my name because if you have a good name, you do not change it and plus my mother would have killed me, and my grandmother.

Secondly, God willing, I hope this is not a personal attack on anyone nor their beliefs. It is my sincerest intention to tell my story as I have been asked of how I came from and where I was to where I am now, as honestly as I can, and as they say, "the chips fall where they may." But the only way anyone will benefit from this is to read with an open mind. As the old adage goes that, a mind is like a parachute, there is only one way that it will work and that is if it is open.

Chapter 1

Christianity by Birth

I was born in a small city called Greenville, South Carolina, which is on the east coast of the United States. I was raised by my grandparents. My mother had stepped out and my father was working two jobs and then he moved to New York to take a job, so I stayed with my grandparents who were both retired. They were very old-fashioned, to say the least. They were very conservative and very much so religious. We were very attached to the church that was at the end of our street. My grandfather was a full-blooded Native American Indian and he was the patriarch – my family has a typical male patriarch figure and my grandmother was the child of Irish immigrants.

There was a lot of religion in my home in the sense that we went to church on Sunday mornings, Sunday evenings, and on Wednesdays. It was a necessity that you sat down at my kitchen table and you would pray before you eat, pray before you sleep, and all of these things. This was very much part of my upbringing. There was no such thing as music at my home other than the music that my grandparents approved of, which was the music that I did not want to listen to whatsoever. There were no girls allowed at my home, no parties. I did not go to school dances; all of these things while my grandfather was still alive. So, I had the typical nerd upbringing, as they say.

The only thing I knew about religion growing up; like most children know is Sunday school. It was pretty much my religious upbringing, which was before the normal church services. I went to a Sunday school where we sang songs, painted pictures, and we learned about Noah and the flood. We learned about Moses and the Children of Israel and Pharaoh and splitting the Red Sea. We also learned the story about David and Goliath, we learned the story about Jesus feeding the 5,000 the loaves of bread and fish, we learned about sermon on the mountain, the crucifixion and the resurrection; this is pretty much the crux of what I knew about my religion growing up.

Then as I got older, my grandparents removed me from Sunday school and took me to the normal Sunday service, which was extremely boring. It was not like what you see on television. We went to a Methodist church and the benches were quite uncomfortable. You stood up and sung a hymn, then you sat down and listen to the preacher, and you repeat these things and that was pretty much it.

Chapter 2

The Thinking Apprentice

All of that somewhat changed at the age of 14. At the age of 14, I started to go to Saturday evening youth services. That was a lot more fun than Sunday school because we played basketball, volley ball and dodge ball. We had pizza, cake, candy and all that good stuff. At the end, for 30 minutes our Youth Pastor – who lived across the street from me – would sit down and give 30 minutes of sermon about religion, God, and something that was beneficial for the youth – the problems and temptations that youths face. I really like the way he presented it – in a bold, fresh, and new type of manner. It was a lot different and a lot more interesting to me.

When I turned 15, I began to attend high school as a freshman. My grandmother could not take me to school because she was battling with cancer at that time, on and off. So she talked to the Youth Pastor's mother to take me to school. It was a big prestige for me to go to school with the Youth Pastor whom I looked up to, knowing that he was the Class President of our school. Not only that; he was a senior and drove a very nice car. So we became friends through that. Even though it was very odd for a freshman and a senior to be in any type of friends.

We became very good friends and he started to take me to other services throughout South Carolina, North Carolina, and Georgia; called Young Life Fellowship. It is an organization of youth, run by youth, put on by youth, and their services were a lot better than any one that I had been to. There was a lot of music involved, there was a lot of very strong biblical preaching based on the bible but it was what they called 'the fire and brimstone' preaching. It was either you do this or this is going to happen based on the biblical principles. Everyone there seemed to have that love of brotherhood and sisterhood that really attracted me. It was very entertaining to me.

At that point of my life when I started to go to retreats, camps, and et cetera I would say I became a religious Christian by choice rather than by upbringing. I fell in love with my religion. I became emotionally attached to my faith. It was at that point that I could say that I became what is known as saved by grace rather than just by birth. All of that was going on for quite a period of time. Then my friend, Benjamin, graduated and I became a sophomore. Then after that he attended a Bible College in my hometown, which is very well-known in the United States amongst religious conservatives (Christians).

It is called Bob Jones University. I would say this is an ultra-conservative university in its biblical principles. There is no such thing as boyfriend and girlfriend in that campus, no men and women mingling, no such thing as men dressing in inappropriate manner – there was a very strict dress code. It is just the way of Bob Jones University. Benjamin wanted to study beyond his field of study, he wanted to focus on textual criticism of the bible. A textual critic is someone who takes the oldest existing documents that we have of the bible today and they try to decipher them through learning their languages – which are very hard languages such as ancient sematic Hebrew, ancient Greek and Latin.

Textual critics have to go through these existing documents which there are now about 7,000 variant documents of what we now know of as the Bible. The textual critic's job is to decipher which one of these documents most accurately represents the original form of the authors' thoughts; because there are no originals. There was also no chain of transmission back to an original which made it very difficult because the documents were written in different languages and have questionable authenticity.

As I was Benjamin's apprentice, I have made up my mind that at the age of 16 that I wanted to go to Bob Jones and I got enrolled into the waiting list. I wanted to be a textual critic, a bible scholar; a pastor. I wanted to be ordained as a minister, a missionary. I began to take missionary courses at a church. I wanted to do it to the best of my ability in all respects.

Chapter 3

Seeking the Truth
with Benjamin

As Benjamin became more involved in his college studies, he was not able to really keep up with his pastoring at our church and also at his Young Life pastoring. Initially, he started allowing me to fill in for him, with the Pastor's approval while they looked for replacement as the Youth Pastor; because the age of 16 was too young. But I started to do some Young Life pastoring as well and apparently people told me that I had the gift – I could speak well with some type of education, people were really intrigued by the way I spoke. I was invited to more Young Life pastoringships. My Youth Pastor was very pleased with what I was doing, so he decided just to leave me for a while in that position.

That was all going fine and dandy until the summer of 1996. It is what I would say where the story really begins to get me to where I am right now. In the summer of 1996, my friend Benjamin came to me and he asked me a question

"Have you ever read the Bible?"

I asked him, "What kind of a silly question was that? I'm doing your job as the Youth Pastor, I'm filling

in your position and you're asking me if I've ever read the Bible; what do you mean?"

"You know what I mean."

"No, I don't. You tell me."

He said, "Have you read the Bible like you read a novel?"

I said, "No, I have not read the Bible Genesis and beginning Genesis one more and read it to Revelation. I didn't really know anyone who had done that in one sitting, beginning to end. Because the Bible is a very deep and complex book to read like that."

Benjamin asked me how is it that we can be telling people that we are preaching God's words and that our goal in life is to preach God's words and the Bible is the acronym of BIBLE (The Basic Instructions Before Leaving Earth) yet we do not know it intimately like this? How can we say that we are preaching the gospel of Christ and we have not read the book revealed by God in this manner?

I said "That's a good question."

He said, "I want to challenge me and you to take this summer of 1996 and read the Bible cover

12

to cover. Sit down; don't skip, don't flip, don't jumble around, start Genesis 1:1 and read it to Revelation. And let's see what God says to us. Because my belief was that God was god, Jesus was god, and the Holy Spirit was the third manifestation of personage of the one triune god, and that personage lived inside of me after accepting Christ as my savior, that Holy Spirit lived inside of me; therefore if I had god inside of me then God's words should speak to me just like it can speak to everyone else."

We then decided to let the Bible speak to us. Let the Bible say what it has to say to us. I thought this was an amazing challenge being that I wanted to do this for my life. This would be a good place to start. To spend a summer intimately getting to know God's words.

Beyond that, I am a perfectionist at heart. I am someone who likes only perfection. If I do something, I am going to do it to the best of my ability. I have a competitive spirit that I'm probably going to try to beat everyone else that I know at it. If I was going to be a Christian, it was going to be the best one I could be. I was going to do everything that I could do within that field. If it meant traveling the world to spread the gospel of Christ, that was what I was going to do. If it meant that I had to study and learn God's word like a bookworm, then that was what I was going to do. Whatever it took, that was what I was going to do.

Beyond that, I started to study martial arts at the age of 14. I became a perfectionist of that. I got one black belt and that was not enough. Then I went to get another black belt and that was not enough. So I got another black belt and that still was not enough. I then opened up two martial arts schools. That was not enough, so I opened up another one in DC, one in New York. That was not enough and it seemed like it never was enough. But this is just the type of personality that I have; they call it a go-getter.

In the summer of 1996, we started and I started at "In the beginning, God created the heavens and the earth." (Genesis 1:1) There were many things that I saw and this is where there is going to be some sensitive information, but I have to give it to you in all honesty and I give it to you as clearly as I can. If I gave you all of the things that I saw that led me to deduce the things that led me to where I am right now, this would be endless. But I want to get to the major points.

Chapter 4

Unfolding Doubts

My friend Benjamin was pointing out to me some things that were very interesting that I did not really comprehend until I actually accepted Islam and began to learn the Quran from the Arabic language. Benjamin noticed there were places in the Old Testament where you could see that the language that was being spoken was inhuman. Meaning that the language was so beautiful, the grammar was so delicate, the prose was so pristine that you could tell it was not the language of human beings.

Then there would be other places within the same Old Testament that you could tell were written by very different authors. They were written in different grammar, with different syntax, with different Hebrew verge verbiage. Some of it was even remedial and some of it was not really a high-status scholarly Hebrew. So you could tell that it was different people who were speaking and there were reasons behind that that we were told because of the different authors that wrote it down and it came to the minds of human beings. Nevertheless, that was what Benjamin was pointing out to me.

What began to catch my attention was the stories of God's prophets throughout the Old Testament. This was what really hit home with me. Growing up, my idea of God's prophets were that they were God's prophets and He chose them because they were the best human beings to guide people to Himself. This was what I saw as a prophet. Someone that was the best of creation because they had to lead people to a righteous way of life. But when I started to read the New Testament, I began to get somewhat of a different picture that is depicted of some of the prophets in the Old Testament. It was hard for me to even relate some of the stories there; even if they are for information purposes.

The first one had to be of course in the beginning in Genesis with Noah (peace be upon him). The story goes that Noah was a man who preached for almost a thousand years and not many people listened to Noah. But Noah was relentless in his preaching until God finally decided that He was tired of the disobedience of human beings and He was going to re-begin His creation anew with those who believed in Him. So He sent the flood and Noah built the ark and saved those who wish to be saved and believed in God in it.

That was a very beautiful story. But there was another story about Noah that happened after the flood that is not really prestigious and in the least of terminologies. The story was something such as Noah realized that if you took grapes and you let them sit for a while, they ferment. It then became a very delicious drink called alcohol. Then Noah decided to drink alcohol and at one point in Genesis, it describes Noah as being drunk, passed out in his home naked.

Someone apparently had to write this so it was known that Noah was someone who drank enough to be passed out at his home naked. This caught my attention because I said to myself this does not really seem to fit with my thought process of a prophet. I know Noah is a human being and I should not have to deal with my thoughts. But Noah was supposed to be God's prophet. I don't know how much credibility I can put on someone whom I can find laid out in their home drunk, naked.

I have known a lot of alcoholics in my day and I have seen only a few that I would say get drunk enough to be passed out in their home naked. And this was Noah. Someone that goes that far, that drinks alcohol to be laying in their home naked must have a problem with it. This was an excess. This was not just casual having a glass of wine or two a day. This was drunkenness. Any way you want to describe it.

It kind of came as a shock to me and what I said to myself in kind of a funny terminology in my mind, I was like, "Wait a minute. Now I know why not many people listened to Noah - hopefully he started this after the flood. But if he started this before the flood, I know why no one listened to Noah because he was someone who was passed out in his house, was found naked and drunk."

I'm sure every city center I have been in the world has the same – you have your drunks who went around getting drunk and passing out on park benches. Now if that same guy or woman jumps up on the park bench the next day and says that God chose me to be a prophet to guide humanity to himself and I'm going to build this huge boat and if you come and get on it, you will be saved, if not you're going to be destroyed. How many of you are going behind this guy and watch him build this ark and get on it? Nobody.

I then said to myself there's something that hit a chord with me that there's something not so right about this story. But I'm a human being, I don't have the right be using my own mind to do these things. I was still trying to see what the Bible was saying to me.

Then I kept reading. Got through many other stories and I got to the story of Lot, whom we as Muslims know in Arabic as Lut. There are some differences between the Bible scholars whether or not Lot was a prophet. A lot of them said he was not a prophet. Regardless, God saw him important enough to put him in His book. So he's worth talking about.

Lot was sent to the people of Sodom and Gamorrah, whom many of you may know. Sodom and Gamorrah was a complete city that was overrun with the sin of homosexuality that was a blasphemy before God. Lot was sent to warn them against this but they did not listen. Then God ended up destroying the city.

There's another story about Lot in the Bible that is not really so prestigious. The story is about Lot and his two daughters. His two daughters were concerned because Lot was growing old and he had no son. He had no one to carry on his lineage. Therefore, his daughters decided to fix the problem. The way they fix the problem was that the oldest daughter got Lot intoxicated one evening and slept with him and became pregnant by him. Then just to make sure that was a 50-50 chance that a son would happen, the youngest daughter did the same thing the next night. She got Lot intoxicated, she slept with him, and then she became pregnant by him.

Now I'm like, "Wow, the story is getting worse and worse by the prophet, or by the story is getting worse." Now we have someone whom we as Muslims called a prophet, he is a prophet of God because a prophet is someone who is chosen by God to give a message to humanity and this is the description of Lot in the Old Testament. We have a prophet of God now committing incest with his daughters.

Now I'm intrigue at the stories of the prophets and I began to read a little more quickly. Even though I am focusing as much as I can, there are parts that I was going over quicker because I did not really see a lot of use for them. There is even a book like the Book of Ruth that I do not even really understand to this day why it is even in the Bible. It is a love story and the word God is not even in the entire book. It is like a romance novel from beginning to end.

However, what caught my attention more than anything and really put as they say, "the straw that broke the camel's back" was the story of Solomon and the story of David. They are some of my favorite stories in the Old Testament. Solomon was known as the greatest king of Israel. He established the Temple Mount; which is what the Jews are attempting to rebuild now in attempts to bring the Messiah. But there is another story about Solomon that is not as prestigious. It is said that Solomon once became so weak in his faith that he worshiped idols. This is in the Old Testament.

They said Solomon turned to the gods of the idol worshipers. So I caught myself and said wait a minute. What about the people who followed Solomon? If they would have followed him in his idol worship, would have they been right or wrong? Because he is God's prophet, by the way. They were supposed to follow him. So if they followed him in idol worship, how could God have punished them?

Then I got to the story of David. The story out of the Bible is very beautiful. Even like the story in the Quran where David approaches Goliath. The dialogue that takes place between David and Goliath is very amazing. But there is another story about David that is not as prestigious, which is the story about David and a woman named Bathsheba.

Bathsheba was a woman of astute beauty of her time and it is said that David saw her one day. He decided that this woman was so beautiful, he had to have her. So he slept with her. The only problem with that story is that she was married to one of the commanders of David's army named Uriah. So David has just committed the sin of adultery, which is punishable by death according to his own law.

David felt bad for what he's done and he decided he needs to fix it. He did not repent to God and seek to become better. He decided the way he was going to fix it was by sending a letter to his army who were fighting in Palestine at the time. In the letter, he says that when the battle becomes fierce for everyone to abandon Uriah and to leave him, so that he dies. He was killed and therefore David was able to have

23

Bathsheba and there was no one who can say anything about it.

This was the point where I stopped and I said okay, enough is enough. Because now not only do we have a prophet that is given to alcohol so much that he was passed out at his home butt naked, we have a prophet who was sleeping with his daughters, we have a prophet who was committing idolatry, and now we have a prophet who was committing adultery and murder. All of these were breaking the first five of the 10 commandments.

There was a huge problem now with me. There was a conflict I have within me. Honestly, these are people that I do not see as prophets and messengers of God. These are like people whom you would see on that show in The States called America's Most Wanted. I had a problem with God's prophets in the Old Testament.

Then I began to ask questions to my pastor about this. I began to ask questions to Benjamin about this. I began to ask questions to my Young Life fellow pastors about this. I even got to talk to a man named Benny Hinn, who was very famous in The States.

But what I was told was the same thing, exactly the same message from most every single individual. That message was,

"Joshua, don't let a little bit of knowledge wreck your faith, because you are not justified by knowledge. You're justified (quoting Paul) by your faith in the Lord Jesus Christ and his shedding of his blood for the redemption of the sins of humanity. And it is that faith and that belief alone which leads one to justification. Not works, not knowledge, nothing else other than faith."

My pastor and a few more had explained to me that this faith is the faith beyond the capability of understanding; faith beyond the capability of reason. This is true faith – it is to believe when even there is no reason to believe. My pastor told me, "Why are you even messing around in the Old Testament?" He kind of got angry with me. He said,

"Old Testament has its value, it has its place for reference. But it is the Old Covenant. The oldest covenant that God had with the Children of Israel. He dealt with them in a different way and manner, and they have their different issues with God. We have now passed from that old covenant into the new covenant of the salvation of Jesus Christ and the cross. We have now passed over into the new covenant of blood shedding and the redemption of sins. Therefore, the old covenant is no longer valid. The way God dealt with Children of Israel is no longer valid for dealing with human beings you must now deal with it under the new covenant of God. So why don't you, if you want to spend all of this energy, why don't you spend it in the New Testament? Why don't you spend it in the life of Jesus Christ? If you want to know someone, know your Lord, know your savior. Know Him intimately and then you will come into redemption. You cannot get redemption in the Old Testament."

I then said "Okay." Because you have to understand that I had my whole life laid ahead of me and it was based on this book. I was starting to see cracks in this foundation and I wanted to seal them up as quickly as possible. So I got through the Old Testament because I made a promise to Benjamin that I would do it beginning to the end. Even though I did see some things that bothered me in the Old Testament.

Chapter 5

The Constant Contradictions

There were some facts that were congruent throughout the Old Testament that were very clear. In the first and foremost fact of the Old Testament that was extremely clear was the message that God was one. This is extremely clear throughout the entire Old Testament, "Hear o Israel, the Lord your God is One." That is still quoted in every synagogue throughout the world today. "Hear o Israel, I am The Lord your God and there is none else" or "Israel, I am The Lord your God and there is none like unto Me." (Mark 12:29) This was very clear over and over again.

It was also clear that God was jealous for only one reason which was His worship. He did not tolerate people worshiping something else besides Him. This was capital crime number one and this was the reason why He punished the Children of Israel at every point that He could. For only one reason – they are worshiping something else other than Him. He did not go along with that as His first commandment was "thou shalt have no other god before me" (Exodus 20:3) – which is not the proper translation of the Hebrew adage.

The correct connotation of the first commandment is God says "you shall have no other God along with Me." (Exodus 20:3) Meaning that you should not make anything equal to Him. This is what God's statement was, you make nothing in My creation as equal as you have Me (God) The Creator. The worship that belongs to God, you give it to nothing else. The sacrifice that God asks to give to Him, you give to Him alone and to nothing else. The obedience that God has for Him, you obey Him and you obey nothing else in creation. This was very clear throughout the Old Testament.

Another thing that was clear about the Old Testament was that if you wanted to go to Heaven, there were two ways to do so. Number one, you worship God alone without anything else. Number two, you obey Him. This was the path of salvation of the Old Testament. You worship God and you obey Him. And when you made a mistake, you turn to Him, you became sorry for your sins, you repented to Him, you showed Him that you were sincere through the sacrifices in such nature and God would forgive. This is very clear. It was kind of interesting to me. The last statement of the Old Testament that God leaves as a bidding farewell of the Old Testament which is in the book of Malachi.

In Malachi, in the last chapter, God says something that is very profound. It says, "I do not change. Therefore the sons of Jacob are not consumed." (Malachi 3:6) What that means is God is telling the Children of Israel, God doesn't change His mind, He doesn't change His opinion, He's not someone who wakes up and feels one way one day and another way another day, and this is the reason He has not destroyed all of you.

Apparently this was my frame of mind going into the New Testament. I began in the New Testament; Matthew, Mark, Luke and John. To give you the historical critical and textual analysis of the New Testament of the first four books which is known as the Gospels, or even the first three which was known not as the Gospels; would take weeks and months and years to give you all of the issues that arise. But I want to do is give you the message that I found. There was a way that I read it that allowed me to see something that I would have never seen before, I never had saw before, and not a lot of people see because of the way that they read it.

Most people read the New Testament, Matthew beginning to end, Mark beginning to end, Luke beginning to end, John beginning to end. What you get through that type of reading is you get four stories seemingly from four different people telling the same story from a different vantage point. This is the general belief. But there was a way I learned to read it from the textual critic professor at Bob Jones University that gave me a completely different image – the linear method of reading.

The linear method of reading is that you read the same story out of Matthew and then you go to Mark and find the same story, you read it. You go to Luke you find the same story and you read it. You go to John and you find the same story and you read it. You do that with every single story that is throughout the life of Jesus Christ. When you read it in that method, you see a completely different picture than what you would normally see. You quickly will come to realize through that type of reading that it is not one story told four different vantage points; it is four completely different stories told by four completely different things who saw and thought four completely different things and whose meaning of Jesus's life was four completely different things.

Nevertheless, what I wanted to focus on was Jesus's life – what did he teach, what did he preach, what was his message, and what did he want to give to humanity. I found out that it was this: Jesus taught about God, that God is one. In the New Testament, Jesus Christ teaches "Hear o Israel, The Lord your God is One." (Deuteronomy 6:4) He quotes this out of Deuteronomy. He taught that God the Father as someone that was greater than Himself. Jesus even said, "I have to go to the Father for the Father is greater than I." He made an analogy that the servant is not greater than the master nor is the Son greater than the Father.

Once a man came to Jesus and asked Jesus, "O good master, tell me how to inherit eternal life." Jesus responded his question with a question. He said, "Why do you call me good?" If you really look into the Greek documents of this verse, what Jesus really said in that terminology is "Why do you call me good for there is only one source of good?" (Mark 10:18) This was what he said. The only source of good in the creation is God.

I was starting to see through Jesus's teachings whom I believed was the second personage of the Trinity – I thought Jesus was god – but I was beginning to think that Jesus is spending a lot of time to not disassociate himself with God but he distinguished himself from the Creator. Jesus said that "This is the eternal life, this is the way to salvation that they may know you the only true God and Jesus Christ whom you have sent." (John 17:3) This was what Jesus has said or all that was left of what he said because the testament's original words of Jesus spoke Aramaic; and we have no documents in Aramaic. The older ones are in Greek and Latin then translated to English. So what we are reading is not what he has speak. Jesus was stated to say, "Yes, I am the way to the truth and life. No one comes unto the Father except through me." (John 14:6)

I was starting to see a Jesus who was uniquely different from the Creator God and he was making this very distinguishable in many places. When someone came and asked Jesus when the Day of Judgment is, he answered "And God is All-Knowing". Jesus said "No one knows about the hour; not even the Son, only the Father in heaven." (Matthew 24:36)

Now I was questioning myself that if Jesus is god, he would know everything as God knows everything. God cannot be all-knowing and not know something at the same time. I was starting to see that the nature of God and the nature of Jesus were quite distinct amongst each other. Also, there were places that were true indeed, Jesus implicitly made statements that can be deduced alone – if you take them alone implicitly to say that he was directly related to God in a form of divinity. But I have quickly learned as a student of psychology that you see that because of you already preconceived notions of what you believe about God. Without that preconceived notion you would see something quite different when you weigh Jesus' implicit statements against his explicit statements that are very clear throughout the New Testament.

Therefore now I had a question in my mind about salvation. What does this mean for salvation if I am now beginning to see from the New Testament that Jesus is not god and he is someone that is distinct from God, and he is someone that taught us that he is distinct from God. Even when he taught us to pray, he said, "Pray thus our Father who are in heaven.." (Ibid. 6:9)

What about salvation? A rich man once asked Jesus about the same issue. This story is very famous, but I saw something completely different when I read it with this notion in my mind – of Jesus being someone who is distinct from God. The man came to Jesus and asked him, "O good master, how do I go to heaven?" Jesus did not tell him, "I'm going to live and die on the cross and shed my blood for the redemption of your sins." Jesus told this man, "Thus follow the commandments." Obey God's law, listen to God, and do what you have to do and you go to heaven. The man says, "I've done that." Jesus saw this opportunity to teach the man a valuable lesson. He said, "If you've done that, then what you need to do is sell everything you own, you need to pick up your burden and follow me." (Matthew 19:6-22) Meaning you need to be doing what I'm doing; if you are so perfect, you need to do my job; why don't you help me? That was when the man realize that he was not fitting to the task and he left crying.

Nevertheless, Jesus told him that if he wanted to go to heaven, he follow the commandments and he did not change it, he left it as thus. He even said that when the disciples were once debating about the commandments which Jesus himself was a practicing the Law of Moses. He taught that the Law of Moses should be obeyed, he taught that he himself was not come to break the law, but to fulfill it. He even told the man and emphasised to him one time, speaking of the Law of God he said that "Whosoever shall break the smallest of the commandments of God and teach men to break the commandments of God, then he would be the worst person in the kingdom of heaven. But whosoever shall obey the least of the commandments of God and then teach people to obey the commandments of God, that person will thus become the greatest person in the kingdom of heaven." (Matthew 5:19) Jesus was highly emphasised on obeying God's law.

When the disciples one day were debating about the commandments – which one was greater – they asked Jesus which is the greatest commandment? We don't find that they asked him but we can tell from what Jesus told them that they asked. He said, "The greatest commandment is thus – which is not any of the 10 commandments – is to love the Lord your God with all of your heart, with all of your might, with all of your strength. And then you love your neighbor like you love yourself. This is the greatest of the commandments." (Mark 12:30-31) He said this is actually what the rest of the commandments hang upon. These are the two fundamental principles of Jesus' religion. Do you want to know what Jesus' religion was? He said it was this. To love the Lord your God, with all of your heart, with all your might, your strength and you love your neighbor like you love yourself.

It is very interesting on the step of just a small side note as I am now working on a Ph.D. on Islamic Law that the fundamental principle of Islamic Law and the religion of Islam is this. There are two sets of principles that everything in Islam hangs upon. The first principle is that you love your God with all your might, your heart, and your strength. You give God His due right of worship. That is one side. On the other side, you love your neighbor as you love yourself. This is Islamic Law. And everything else descends from these two principles. Every law that you can find in Islam fits in one of these two categories. Either the rights that you give to The Creator or the rights that you give to the creation. This was what Jesus himself is teaching.

Thus I began to question myself and I'm saying that wait a minute, I'm was finding that Jesus in the New Testament that taught the God was the greatest thing in creation. That you worship Him and obey Him and you go to heaven. This was what I found God teaching in the Old Testament. So what about the salvation, the crucifixion; where are all of these now sitting and resting? And how do they rest on this point?

I started to read the crucifixion stories out Matthew, out of Mark, out of Luke, and out of John. I did not really realize the point in the beginning, first reading through the first four Gospels, because I was conflicted. Here is seemingly a Jesus who came to live a life and died on a cross, shed his blood for the redemption of sins that are implicit verses in the New

Testament that said this was Jesus saying that this is why I am here – to shed my blood for the redemption of your sins – but yet when the people came to him and told him that they are going to crucify you, we find the Jesus who is unwilling. So unwilling that he took his disciples went to the garnet Gethsemane, told them you stand here and watch so that nobody can get me, I'm going down here. He falls on his face, he prays so hard that his sweat becomes as drops of blood and his prayer is not for strength, his prayer is not for the ability to be able to withstand the punishment that he is coming upon. No. His prayer was, "God, if it be let this cup pass from me." (Matthew 26:39) Meaning, God do not let them crucify me.

I was very conflicted about this Jesus who was supposed to be crucified for the sins of humanity. Why was he reluctant to take this mission? I could not figure it out. Until I started to read the writings of Paul – which I have read before, but I was reading the way a completely different frame of mind during the challenge. When I got to the book of Galatians, the light bulb turned on for me and it all fell into place.

Chapter 6

Unfolding Truths

First of all, I found out that Paul puts himself directly at contradiction with the teachings of Jesus Christ. Paul taught that the law – God's law – was not a method in a salvation. He spent a lot of time doing this. That God's law was not a method in the salvation that it should not be followed, that it should be abandoned and people who come into Christianity that are not Jews should not follow God's law.

Paul even wrote a letter called Galatians – which is to the church at Galatia. He begins the letter by saying, 'O you foolish Galatians, why are you still following this accursed of law?' (Galatians 3:1) And all I could remind myself of was Jesus saying that whosoever shall break the lease of commandments and then teach people to break the commandments would be the worst on this kingdom of heaven. But Paul says something very profound in Galatians. He says that Christ was crucified and cursed; he was cursed according to the law. In order to remove us from the curse of the law for it is written – everything that hangs on a tree is cursed – and it was quoting Deuteronomy. So I was like, wait a minute, why did Paul go to this link to explain this crucifixion as a curse to remove us from the curse of the law.

Then I started to read Deuteronomy – the Jewish law. What happened was all of the light bulbs fell into place. In Deuteronomy, God teaches that if you crucify a criminal which is the worst capital punishment that you can have in in Judaism, to hang them but do not let them stay on the cross overnight. If they are not dead, you break the legs, you let them die but you take them down that night and you bury them that night, for everything that hangs on a tree is cursed. I talked to some rabbis and some Hasidic Jewish leaders and they said that the reason why is because the person who is crucified as a criminal, according to God's law they are cursed individuals in this life and whatever it is in the next life is not for them. They are done. These people will never see the Kingdom of God. It all hit home for me.

I now know why they wanted to crucify Jesus. I now know why Jesus did not want to be crucified and I now know why crucifixion was not a method in the salvation. Number one, Jesus came to a people who were the Children of Israel – forgotten and completely abandoned God's true message. There was a group of them called the Pharisees and Sadducees, which Jesus said that were murderous and adulteress nation.

They had become so entrapped in the law that they completely forgot about the spirit of the law and the spirit of religion – having connection with The Creator. They actually turned religion into a way to get rich. They were using religion in a way to subjugate human beings. They were making themselves prestigious and using the law to subjugate everyone else. Jesus came to put that down. He came to knock them off their pedestal, to show them for who they were, and to put people back on the level footing with God. And he himself even told them this many times.

Jesus came to show the Children of Israel that God's law was sent in order to help human beings live a life according to God's pleasure and to please Him, not for them to please themselves. He did this with walking to the corn field on the Sabbath and the other things that he did. He was trying to show them this. This was the problem of the Jews – the Pharisees and Sadducees. Number one, Jesus was not the Messiah they were hoping for. Their Messiah they were looking for was the Messiah that will come and sit on the throne of Solomon and rule the world with an iron fist in the law of Judah. This was what they were looking for in the Messiah.

However, this was not found in Jesus. Jesus was renouncing the world at every chance he could get. They did not like that. But Jesus was trying to explain to them that I have not come to bring you the kingdom of this world; I have come to bring you the kingdom of heaven. That was what I have come to do. But they were not trying to hear that. Because they have become so attached to this world they did not want to leave, that the only success was in this world.

That was not the worst crime though. The worst crime that Jesus committed was that he challenged the status of those who were in authority. He challenged their position, their system, or the status-quo of the people who were using the law to subjugate human beings. I don't care what your message is, I don't care how good of the message you have, I don't care how good of a human being you are; the moment your message become the direct threat to those in authority, to those who are using their power and prestige to subjugate human beings, you will become public enemy number one. Jesus put himself in this position. So what happened? They get rid of him.

They had to get rid of him. So if you look at the New Testament the first four Gospels, there are many places where the Jews tried to trap Jesus in his own words in order to get him to look like a fool, in order to disgrace him in front of the people, and many times they even try to put himself at direct odds with the ruler of the day, Caesar.

One time, they asked him to trick him, "Should we pay taxes to Caesar?" Had Jesus said "No", that is capital crime. Automatically Caesar would have his head chopped off on the spot. What did Jesus say? He tricked them back. He said give to God what belongs to God; and give to Caesar what belongs to Cesar. (Matthew 22:21) They got very angry. There were many times they tried to trap his words but they were unable to do so. They then decided to do was not only do they need to get rid of him, but they could have killed him. Jesus had no tribe, no lineage, and no father. He had no one to support him. But killing him would not kill his message.

What they wanted to do was discredit Jesus and his message. There was one sure way to do that. It was to crucify him. Because they knew if we can crucify Jesus as a criminal according to the law and crucify him according to the very law he was saying he is coming to fulfill, we can now crucify him as a criminal according to it and curse him as a criminal according to it, he will look like the biggest fool on the face of the earth. This was their goal.

There were different ways to do that. Number one, they started saying that Jesus was calling himself the King of the Jews. When he was saying that he was the King of the Jews, it directly put him at threat to Caesar's rule. Because he was not necessarily calling himself God or Son of God that got him crucified. Because the person who went on the cross, when they nailed the sign above the cross, it said, 'Here lies the King of the Jews'. This was the biggest crime they were pushing against him.

They were using some of the things Jesus said to deduce that he was putting himself at the divine nature with God, which is a capital crime under the Jews law. When they went to Pilate, they took these threat to him and even Pilate himself after inquiring about Jesus, he said I don't see any fault in this man; what do you want me to do with him? What was their response? "Crucify him." This is the only way we can get rid of him and his message.

When Jesus found out that they were going to crucify him, what did he do? He went to the Garden Gethsemane, he fell on his face and he prayed for God to remove him from this mission. He said "Do not let them crucify me". Because Jesus understood that if they crucify him, they will never believe in him. Jesus was only sent to the lost sheep of the house of Israel. That is a very important fact. "My Father, if it is possible, let this cup pass me by; nevertheless, not as my will but as you will." This was his prayer in the Garden Gethsemane. (Matthew 26:39)

Indeed now I was starting to realize why Jesus did not want to be crucified, why he cannot be crucified. I realized that had he been crucified, he would have been a liar according to his own law. He would have not fulfill the Law of Moses. He would have actually been a criminal according to the Law of Moses and he would have been a cursed individual, which Paul says he was. He was crucified as a criminal and he was accursed according to his law. But this was not the message of Jesus Christ.

Chapter 7

Point of No
Return

I started asking a lot of these types of questions to my pastor. He removed me from being the youth minister. I did not want to be a youth minister anymore anyway because I could not see myself preaching a message that I no longer saw as valid. So I began to ask many questions that finally led me to the textual critic professor of Bob Jones University.

What the textual critic professor told me was, "Joshua, the bible that you have is the products of the hands of men and women. That has been passed down over thousands and thousands of years and copied by the hands of men and women who copied it by hand in the most remedial forms in its early stages. During that copying, they made many mistakes. Some of them purposely, many of them without purpose. But there were changes that were made and they were not able to be corrected and we lost the originals and there is no way to know what we really have anymore. So the scholars of the bible do the best that they can to try to find out what is really said. But the end result of what you have is a book written by the hands of men and women that they left their fingerprints on. And it is not perfect.

But the people who believed in it, believe in it by faith. And it is that faith which takes them to the justification and salvation. It is that faith alone without the capacity of reason that leads one to salvation."

This was where I stopped him. I said, "You know what. I'm not going for that anymore. Number one, because God gave me an intellect for a reason. He created logic in human beings for a reason to understand the world around them and that logic should indeed again make them understand Him. Number two, "God is perfect, right?"

He said, "Yes."

I said, "Therefore, everything emanating from Him should be perfect. His prophets should be perfect. They should show us the right way to live a life; not the wrong way. His book should be perfect. The books of the Old Testament are not perfect. They do not show us the right way; they show us the wrong way to live. The book that I have in my hand is not perfect. The religion you are telling me to believe in is not perfect because it does not agree with the same logic and reason that God gave me to understand Himself. Therefore it cannot be from God."

And I left Christianity at that point.

I said that I believe in God. There is no fool in his right mind is going to get me to deny that The Creator existed. The world around me is enough evidence for the existence of a designer. But I did not know the right way He wanted from me. So I started to study other religions. I studied Hinduism, Buddhism, Taoism, Judaism, everything I could get my hands on. What I found was much what I found in Christianity. Because there was one thing that I wanted. From now on, there was only one way I was going to accept another religion – it had to come with proof that was just as perfect as the religion says it is.

My grandfather told me something when I was young and I remember it. He said, "Young man, the truth will always come with proof. Therefore if someone says they are telling you the truth, ask them for some proof." So I asked for proof in each religion I studied. What I found was none of the proof that was perfect. All of them had their proofs that they said you should believe this and that, but when you boil it all down, every other religion always had to come to the point that you just have to believe it. You just have to believe it even if you do not understand it. I was not going down that road.

I had even been mocked quite a few times; even in my face once by a pastor who told me,

"You just showed yourself how big of a fool you are to tell me that you studied the world's religion in a period of a year. It cannot be done, so you are showing me that you did not do it."

I said, "No, what I'm showing you is that I have some common sense. If you go to a refrigerator and you pull out the carton of milk and you take a sip of it and the milk is sour, do you keep drinking the glass?"

No. You don't drink the glass in hopes that the last sip of milk is going to not be sour. You trash the glass and the carton of milk. That's all it took for me, a sip. When I tasted the sourness, I discarded the milk. What I was looking for was the good milk.

After all of this, I read some of the Torah, some

of the Bhagavad Gita, the Vedas you could not read in a lifetime, the scrolls of Tao, the books of Confucius, the teaches of Buddha – not to insult but I don't know why Buddha is a religion. Buddha never mentioned God. He does not mention God whatsoever. I studied the book of Wiccan, the book of Spells, the Bushido code of conduct. What I found in them there were a lot of beneficial teachings mixed with things that only way you can believe in them is you take that logic that God gave you and you turn it off.

I read a book about Islam in a public library. The book about Islam said that Muslims were Arabs who worshipped the moon God called Allah, who lives in a box in the desert Saudi Arabia and that they had many wives whom they beat regularly and that the greatest duty of a Muslim was to kill a non-Muslim and it was a religious duty and if they did so they would be granted with virgins in heaven.

Consequently, I put the book about Islam up and I said to myself I have read about some crazy religions before, but this one has to take the cake. And if I ever meet a Muslim, I will beat him up and

I will call the FBI. But I lived in South Carolina and I have never seen a Muslim in my life. I have seen some in New York visiting my dad but you stand at the other side of the street and they did not bother you, you do not bother them.

Chapter 8

Life of Purpose

At that point I gave up religion. I gave up even looking for God at the age of 17 years old. I don't know if any of you know if a 17 year old who is frustrated with God and religion and his parents and all of that, there is a lot of trouble he can get into. And again, I am a perfectionist. So I was going to do the best I could to get into the most trouble I could. In a very short amount of time, I started getting into a fight was my big problem. I had to work on my second black belt at that time. I was ready and willing to show anyone who challenged me that I could give you Kung Fu connection right on the spot.

I really didn't need a reason to get my frustration out. I got kicked out of school. I ended up making a lot of enemies. That way of life was not working out well for me. I lost a 4-year scholarship once in a Clemson university to play baseball. So I was going down the wrong road very fast. My grandmother had no idea what to do. She was trying to get me all kinds of counseling, sent me to the youth camp and stuff like this but I ran away from the camp.

There were two things that changed that that brings us to the end. The first one was that I was

coming home from a party at Clemson University. Since I got kicked out, I could not attend, I was going to make my name known at Clemson University. I was coming back from a party and my friend and I were highly intoxicated. He was driving and he fell asleep at the wheel. We flipped the car over and over again on Highway 85 in South Carolina. We totaled the car so much that it broke into pieces – one part was in the median and the other part was in the ditch.

When I woke up, I woke up to the ground being up and the sky being down. The car flipping. You know you don't really think then you just realize you need to get out of the car. I have seen Hollywood movies that when the car flips what's the next thing that happens; it blows up. So I got out and I dragged my friend out. I took assessment of myself and I realised that this car was destroyed but my friend only had a broken ankle and I only had a very small cut in my arm. That was it. We walked away from the accident.

When the State Trooper came and took us to the hospital and my friend to jail, he said, "Young man, God has a purpose for you two. There is a reason why you are here today. I've been to too many accidents and this one neither one of you should have walked away from. God has a reason for you to be here, you need to figure out what it is."

I laughed in the back of my mind. I said, "You know what God, if you wanted to find me, You had your chance." So I looked at my friend and said God must have a purpose for you and I'm just glad that I was with you tonight so we didn't both die. But I did not listen. A couple of weeks later – maybe a month or two later – me and the same friend went to New York. We decided to go to New York. I told my grandmother I was going to sleep at his house, he told his mother he was going to sleep at my house. Then we went to New York.

In New York, I went to the ATM to get some money out. When I turned around, there was a guy with a gun pointing directly at me. He did not say "give me the money". He was really needing this money I supposed. Because he looked at me directly in the eye, pulled the trigger of the gun. I thanked my martial arts training at that time that I just quickly reacted and jumped on him. We both smashed on the glass door of the ATM station. I told my friend we have got to go. So we left to South Carolina and I did not tell anybody what happened.

I did not tell my grandmother what happened and I started to have some very bad nightmares about these two incidences. But the incidences ended quite differently. They ended with my death. It is very rare that you die in dreams and see what happens after you die. In both of these dreams I died and I passed over into the next life and there was something that was waiting for me on the other side of death. However, I would wake up screaming.

My grandmother finally asked me after a couple of nights "Why are you screaming at night?" I told her what happened. She told me, "God has a purpose for you. If you don't realize God has a purpose for you, you are the biggest idiot I have ever seen in my life. And I did not raise an idiot. So you need to get out there and find out what has happened. You're lucky your grandfather is not alive because he would beat you to death here at this kitchen table. If you don't listen to God, you're going to hell. This is a warning to you."

I told her that I looked for God and I did not find Him. She did not tell me to go to church. She told me, "God doesn't go anywhere. You just have not found Him."

So I became a deist at that point in my life, which is someone who believes in God but they just have no religion. Something changed about me at that time. I stopped looking for God and I get on my hands, knees and prayed as how all the religious books have taught me. I get on the ground and I ask at this point of my life, "God, if You want me to know the truth, then You need to guide me. If You want me to know about You and Your way of life, what You want from me, then here is Your opportunity. I'm here, I'm not going anywhere. You can leave me a message. I need some help here."

Chapter 9

The Friday Prayer

I started to clean up my act – become a better person. It was not really that easy. You do not change overnight, but I was attempting to. It just so happen that after that, few months after that, I met a Muslim who was a friend of mine. I never knew he was a Muslim. I had been to his house on many occasions after school. There was a couple of reasons why I never knew he was a Muslim.

I was at his house one day and we were debating about religion. I did not know he was a Muslim for two reasons. Number one, he was African American. I thought that all Muslims were Arabs. His name was Musa, but we called him Blunt. He was from New York. I did not know that he could sell drugs, which is what he was doing for living.

I was sitting there with another friend debating something and he came up and asked, "You ever heard about Islam?"

I said, "Yes, I have heard all about it."

"Well, I'm a Muslim."

"Wait a minute. You cannot be a Muslim."

He asked why.

"Because you're black."

"I'm real Muslim."

I told him what I read. He said what I read was completely garbage.

So I said, "Then you tell me about Islam."

He said he couldn't.

I asked why not.

He said, "Because I am not the best Muslim. But I do know where you can go to find out about Islam. Come with me on Friday to the mosque for Jumuah."

The only thing I heard from that sentence was Friday.

I asked what is mosque. He said a mosque is like our church and Jumuah is like Sunday service but no chairs. So I went back and asked my grandmother if she knew there were Muslims living near us. She said yes but they did not bother anybody, so we do not bother them. Then I told her I am going to the mosque on Friday for prayer. She said, "Okay, just be careful."

I went and I have some street sensibility about myself. I have learned a few things in the street life. I did not just ran up into the mosque. I went and sat outside the church. Because the church and the mosque shared the same parking lot. I was watching who goes into the building. Lo and behold, Arabs after Arabs; maybe some Pakistanis, but at that time every Muslim looked same to me. There was a few Africans go into the building, but they were not African Americans.

Then I said to myself, "Check number one; All Muslims are Arabs except for maybe a few Africans."

I was paging Musa because he was not showing up. He was not calling me back. But I was sitting there and then a guy pulled up in front of me and parked. He got out and he asked "How can I help you?" Because he saw me looking at everybody. I said, "Yeah, Musa invited me to come and watch your Friday prayer." He was very soft spoken. He said, "Oh yes, we know Musa. He does not come that much. But, come in. We will take care of you. Anything we can do for you. Please come."

He was kind of not taking "no" for answer. I was kind of suspicious about how enthusiastic he was to take me inside. But I did not see anyone that went into the building that I think I couldn't take two or three of them at a time. So I went in and they gave me a chair at the back of the mosque. I was the only person on the chair. There was this huge group of Arabs in front of me and then there is a curtain. I did not see any women come in. However, I heard chatters of women's voice behind the curtain and I guessed they went inside from the back. I questioned why the women were behind the curtain and why didn't I see them coming in? I thought to myself, it must have been all the bruises they had to hide.

Therefore I was just sitting there and this is where my spider sense starts going off. Like Spiderman, when he is in danger, he tingles. I started tingling. I said to myself, "Wait a minute. You've been set up before to get jumped which if you fight a lot of people you make enemies. It kind of felt like this." And then I was thinking "Why is Musa not here?" Then I remembered he has always talked about going to up to New York and getting that Arab money. I was surprised, this guy Musa must have been working with these Arabs and he sells us Americans to them so they can do their Friday jihad. It's over for me. I'm the sacrificial lamb here and I thought Musa was setting me up.

I started thinking how I can get out of there so they won't kill me. I said to myself, "You know that it's really going to look odd if I go to walk through all of these guys." I thought of exiting through the women's section but I knew that was not a smart idea and for all I know, that's where all the swords or weapons could have been hidden too. As I was thinking, the Imam gets up on this stairs. I said to myself I'll try to go when everybody is focused on him. Because I did not see the guy who brought me in – he was too sweet – just for me to see him get up and start telling people to kill me; could not imagine him doing that.

The Imam then got up on this stairs and he started his sermon. He began with, *"Innalhamdalillahi wa nasta`iduhu..."* until the end of the opening in Arabic. I was thinking, "Oh my god, he was telling them to kill me!" He was yelling in Arabic, pounded his staff, and he pointed in my direction. So I was starting to plan how am I getting out from the mosque? I was really freaking out at this point even though all my imaginations of the possible scenarios were going wild and were quite ridiculous.

Then this Imam started to translate what he said. His translation was that "All praise belongs to God, The Creator of all that exist. We praise Him alone, we seek His help alone, we ask for His forgiveness alone. We seek refuge with God the Creator from the evil that lies within souls of human beings and from our evil deeds. And whomsoever God guides to the truth, cannot be misguided from Him. And whomsoever God leads astray from the truth, cannot be guided back to the truth except by God. I bear witness that nothing has right to be worshiped except The One true God and I bear witness that Muhammad is indeed the prophet and messenger of God."

"Wow!" That was my reaction inside. He caught me my attention really quick with that. Because I had never heard that type of rhetoric anywhere. Not in that pros. I never heard it like that and it was the last thing I expected to come out of the mouth of a Muslim.

Next I think okay, let's see what he has to say. His whole sermon that day was on the forgiveness of God. The forgiveness of God is open to any individual, at any place, at any time without discretion. And that there are only three ways that the human being cannot be forgiven by God. He said the first way is if you worship something other than God knowingly. God does not forgive that. After you know the truth, if you worship something other than God, He does not forgive it.

He said number two, the only way you cannot be forgiven is if your soul has reached your throat – meaning that death has come to you. He said the third way was if the sun has risen from the west – which I did not understand meant that the Day of Judgment has begun.   He said but other than that, God forgives everything.

The Imam quoted a story of Prophet Muhammad (peace be upon him) and Angel Gabriel and that discourse they had in the desert. The discourse was that Angel Gabriel came and told him, "Tell the Muslims that God has told them that if they steal, God would forgive them." So he would go and tell them if you steal, God would forgive you. They asked, "What if we commit fornication? What if we commit murder?" and so on and so forth. Every time they would ask a new question, The Prophet would have to go back to Angel Gabriel and he was told to tell them that God will forgive them of that too. Finally Angel Gabriel came back from God and he told Muhammad (peace be upon him), "Tell the Muslims that God has told them this. That no matter what they have done, no matter how great the amount of sins they have committed, even if they stretch as far as the oceans, that as long as they have not worshiped another god along with God knowingly, He will forgive all of it."

I was just amazed. This is the God of The Old Testament. This is the God of Jesus Christ that I know. Where did they get this from? Because they were quoting things that I have never heard before. So after that they get up and they line up wall to wall. Then somebody comes to me and said, "We're going to pray."

I said, "Pray to who?"

He said, "Pray to God the Creator of all that exist."

When they started to pray, the Quran was recited. That did not mean anything to me at first because it sounded just like some good singing. But when the Muslims bow and they prostrate their faces on the ground that started ringing to me. Verses out of the bible, verses out of the Bhagavad Gita, verses out of different religious scriptures when it describes men of God praying and prophets of God praying, they prayed like this. Jesus prayed like this. Abraham prayed like this.

I said to myself, they are not praying, they are worshiping. There is a difference. They are not praying, they are worshiping The Creator of all that exist on their face on the ground. I knew there is no more humble position to be before your Creator than this. This is the way people bow before kings and the emperor.

Chapter 10

The Declaration of Faith

After the Friday prayer, I went to the Imam. The Imam did what we Muslim always do to call people to our religion. He said the five pillars of Islam are these and the six pillars of Iman are these. I told him, "Look here, not to be rude, but there is nothing you are going to tell me is going to make me believe in your religion. I'm not being rude, but I've heard it all. I just have one question for you. Do you have proof to verify your truth? Do you have something that you can put right here in my hands to say what you believe is true?"

He smiled really big. He said "Come with me." He took me to his office and he pulled a book off his shelf and he put it in my hands. I looked at it and it said The Holy Quran. He said this is the proof. Then he started to tell me that the Quran was revealed to Muhammad (peace be upon him). I said, "Look, if your book is what you say it is, it will say for itself." It did not look like a big book. It was not very large. I said "So let me read it and it will say what it has to say on its own.

I took the Quran home and I started to read in on Friday night. I started with the first chapter which seemed to me like the Lord's prayer of the bible. Very similar. What caught my attention more than anything and made me really want to read that book was the second verse of the second chapter. The second verse of the second chapter said this, "This is the Book that has no doubt in it. No discrepancies, no contradictions, no wrong. And it is a guidance for those who fear God." (Surah Al-Baqarah: Verse 2)

I was thinking, "Really?" That was really one of the boldest statements I had ever seen in a religious book make of itself. I said, you know what, I found discrepancies in every book. I will find it in this book. I will find it.

My initial reading of the Quran was to find discrepancies to it to disapprove it. Then I began to read Chapter 2, Chapter 3, Chapter 4, Chapter 5, and in Chapter 2 there is even more things that is coming about what God is saying, "If you are in doubt about this revelation, then find any discrepancies." (Surah Al-Baqarah: Verse 23) Wow, this is getting serious. This is like a direct threat to me.

There was another one that says, "If you are in doubt about this revelation, bring one something like it and call everyone you wish to help you do it; and God says if you cannot do it (which you cannot) then you need to fear My fire whose fuel will be men and stones." (Surah Al-Baqarah: Verse 24) I thought this was real heavy.

I then started to read Chapter 2, Chapter 3, Chapter 4, Chapter 5, and I started to notice names that I recognize. I noticed Noah, Lot, Abraham, Moses, David, Zechariah, John the Baptist, Jesus. Wait a minute, I know all of these people and I have read about them before. But there was something different about these people in this book.

The people in this book; Noah was the greatest human being of his time. He did not do the things which he was telling other people not to do. He lived a life that was pleasing to God in order to show people how to live a life that was pleasing to God. So was Abraham. So was Lot. So was Noah. So was Moses. So was David. So was Zechariah. So was John the Baptist and so was Jesus. They were all at the highest peak of morality. They were all at the highest echelon of caring and they lived the message that they preached. I looked at these people in this book and I said these are prophets. These are messengers. They delivered the message not only with their speech, but with their actions. They did not do the thing which we have all heard before – Don't do as I do but do as I say. They did what they said what they were supposed to be doing.

When I read the Nativity of Jesus Christ story in the Quran, it overshadowed any Nativity story that I had ever read. When I read three chapters of the Quran; Chapter 3, Chapter 17, and Chapter 19, every single question I had about the life of Jesus Christ was answered without question. By the time, I was addicted to the book. It took me three days. Sunday night I got to Chapter 114.

When I put down Chapter 114 and closed the book, I was by myself on Sunday night and I did have tears in my eyes. I said to myself that this is the Book. It has no doubt in it and it is a guidance for those who fear God. This is the evidence. This is the proof. This is the truth. I said I want to be a Muslim. I don't care what it is, I don't care what else they believe. If they follow this Book, then they are on the right path. Because this book is the proof.

This book is a tangible evidence that I could not find fault within my first reading. And after my hundredth, two hundredth, three hundredth reading, I still have not been able to find the fault nor has anyone been able to find the fault in 1400 years it has existed. Many people have tried and they have failed.

I then went back to the Imam on Monday and the door was locked. They told me he lives right behind the mosque. Then I went to his house, I knocked on the door. And I told him I want to be a Muslim. He was shocked. I said your book said everything that it needed to say. So he called some people and had them come over. He said so you believe that there is only one God that is worthy of worship. I said I have always believed that. He said but to be a Muslim you have to also believe in the messengership of Muhammad (peace be upon him).

He started to tell me about Muhammad (peace be upon him). I said I only have one question for you about Muhammad. "Did he give us this book?" He said yes. I said then he is a prophet. That is it. If he gave us this book, then he is what you say he is. That is all the evidence I need because God is perfect, this

Book is perfect, therefore the conduit for the in-between has to be just as perfect because you do not pour clean water through a dirty glass and get clean water at the other end.

I said, "I want to be a Muslim."

So I said, "This day I bear witness that there is nothing that has the right to be worshiped except The One true God, The Creator of all that exist and Muhammad is indeed a Messenger of God just like all the other messengers."

I entered into Islam on this day. This was in December 1998.

I tell my story all throughout the world just for the simple fact that I do not want anyone to be struggling and have to struggle that wants to know the truth about God and His message for humanity. I do not want anyone to have to go through what I went through because there are very simple things that could have happened that I would have never have been here.

The only reason I am here is because God willed it to be so. And because He has given me the opportunity, I feel like sharing that gift – which is to know Him intimately. I know who He is in reality and to be able to worship Him in a way that He wants me to worship Him and be pleasing to Him. This is Islam.

This is the religion of Islam in its entirety. I do not care what you have heard about Islam. I do not care what the media say about Islam. I do not care what any Muslim has told you about Islam. I guarantee that most of it is not Islam. Because Islam is so simple that if it takes more than two minutes to explain it to you, time is wasted. Islam is very simple. It is the message that was initiated with the creation.

When God created the heavens and the earth, He created them perfectly. Within that perfect creation, God decided to create His greatest creation ever. He named that creation Adam. It was the greatest thing He ever created. Because it was the only thing He had ever created that had a choice of to whether or not to worship Him. He told Adam that this is what I want from you. I want you to worship Me and obey Me.

After that creation, came the rest of creation. He created Eve from Adam and from those two the rest of human beings. The message that Adam passed down to his children was this: God is one, you worship Him, and you obey Him you go to heaven. Human beings stayed in that path for a while until they forgot. Then when they forgot, God sent them someone else. He named him Noah. Noah told the creation that God is one, worship Him, obey Him and you go to heaven.

Every time God's prophet would leave, the people would stay on this path for a while until they forgot. They lost the message, lost the books, lost the writings. So God would send somebody else. But all of them had the same message. Do your research.

And then God decided to end His message to the creation to finalize it. So he sent the final Messenger, Muhammad (peace be upon him). Muhammad's message was simple: Worship God alone as one, obey Him and you go to heaven. God's wisdom there is no need to explain why Muhammad was the last messenger. It is very simple. He is the last messenger because his message still exists in its purest form.

That is why the Quran is the last message. We still have the Quran in its purest form. This is why Muhammad's miracle is the greatest miracle, which is the Quran.

Jesus' miracles even though they were some of the greatest that ever existed – he healed the blind, he raised the dead to life – Moses miracle was that he split the Red Sea, Noah's miracle was the ark, Abraham's miracle was all of these things, but Muhammad's miracle is the Quran and it will always be to the Day of Judgment. This is his proof and his evidence for who he was and why he is the last messenger. This is Islam in its entirety. Everything else is just additional to this message. So this is the message of Islam in its purest form.

This is how I got from what I was to where I am now.

Discussions
(Q&A)

QUESTION:

Is Prophet Muhammad far greater than Jesus?

ANSWER:

As a Muslim, we believe that all prophets of God, we believe them equally. We believe that some of them have different statuses and level. We also believe there is a group of them that had a much higher status because God gave them new laws and messages. We believe that Prophet Muhammad (peace be upon him) is the greatest of messengers as he is the last; Seal of Prophets. However, it does not deduct our belief from any other messengers in any way as we cannot be a Muslim if one decides to believe on certain prophets only.

QUESTION:

How does the Trinity deduce to the submission of God is One?

ANSWER:

This question is a question that cannot be answered. We don't know who was the first person to come up with this belief. Paul was one of the ones that promulgate it the most but how it came to be formulate as a doctrine, it can be found. However, it is something that cannot be explained.

QUESTION:

The Quran from the first revelation to this day was also transmitted through human just as the scriptures of other religion are also transmitted through individuals. How is the Quran claimed to be exactly the same as how it was first revealed?

ANSWER:

With the evidence we have left on this day, if we take the Quran and look at it today, it is exactly the same throughout the world. The Quran was passed by companions throughout the world who memorised it directly from Prophet Muhammad (peace be upon him) and it is exactly the same to the letter. The transmissions of memorisers and their teachers are traceable from the current day until the Prophet Muhammad (peace be upon him) himself. Unlike the Bible and all other scriptures, the chain of transmission is lost where it produced multiple versions. Why? Because it wasn't the last message and God didn't intend for it be preserved; unlike the Quran (Surah Al-Hijr: Verse 9).

QUESTION:

Do you (Yusha Evans) believe that Jesus was crucified and died?

ANSWER:

No. I do not believe it since during my studies of the bible before I became a Muslim and also after I became a Muslim because Jesus was not crucified, but he was taken to God; just like Elijah was ascended for his second return. We believe Jesus will return and make clear of he was and what he believed.

Notes